From Both Sides: A Memoir

Ellen Weisberg

Dedicated with love to my mom

Part 1

I was asked on several occasions if I or "they" (the medical doctors) knew how I got cancer, as though it was likely to be anything obvious that I could have avoided if I'd been more careful. I understood where the questions had come from, and that people get scared when they see others falling victim to fate that they themselves could fall victim to at any time. I completely got the fact that it was more comforting for people to hear something along the lines of... I worked every day in a laboratory chock full of carcinogens and teratogens and otherwise nasty, toxic stuff. Or... I had a deplorable diet. Or... I frequently camped out near toxic waste dump sites. Or it was something that I saw on Amazon that I really wanted, and I had ordered it special using a promo code. People seemed to want or need to believe that there was a driving force behind the affliction, something that I opted into... whether knowingly or unwittingly.

So having an understanding of the source of the morbid curiosity, I resisted the temptation to be snarky or defensive and just simply said that I think cancer develops in different people for different reasons. I believe for some, it's mostly genetic predisposition. I liked using Jughead from Archie Comics or Shaggy from Scooby Doo analogies, examples of characters that probably ate as much as Fat Albert but differences in their virtual metabolism kept the first two from getting fat. We all have our inheritance of good and bad stuff inside us dictating how our cells are going to behave over time, and maybe in some cases this is all there is to the story, and you could live like someone with bubble boy disease and still get cancer because you tested positive for the same villain gene that caused your aunt Fanny's lymphoma. Maybe for certain people, over time, the aging cells, which are constantly dividing and making mistakes that typically get corrected, fail to correct themselves because of a faulty DNA repair system. Or over time a person's immune response doesn't fend off the evil doers as well as it used to. Maybe it's mostly the result of an accumulation of "hits" from the environment, each one alone slightly increasing the odds of developing a malignancy and together creating an ominous maelstrom from which there was no escaping. The famous researcher Burt Vogelstein published a paper describing cancer as a result of random mutations, just bad luck.

All I knew in my case was that my mother had battled a more extensive version of the same kind of hormone-responsive cancer that I had, except in her case she was around 15 years older than me at the time of her diagnosis. I also had learned from cousins I'd confided in that my father's side of the family was riddled with cancer. And so I couldn't rule out the possibility that there was something of a hereditary nature making me more susceptible to it. I'd also heard many times that stress can do quite a number on the body, and as I was not exactly a Type B personality, I similarly couldn't eliminate as a candidate my inability to just let things flow and be chill. All taken together, it could have been just about anything that got me to where I was, and apart from being more cognizant of what I was taking into my body and what I was doing with my body, I was at a loss as to how I could have prevented myself from getting sick.

The past year for me had cut deeply. It taunted me with the realization that time was getting shorter as I was moving through it. More so than ever before, I found myself dissecting and analyzing how I was spending my time and with whom I was spending my time. Because in the past year, I was pulled away from the leukemia research and studies I had been dutifully doing at the bench to become someone else's experiment in the same cancer hospital. And in the past year, my life had changed in ways that I never expected, and knew would never reverse.

That first instance of irreversible change was one I'd find myself relaying to people over and over again, like a Vietnam War veteran recounting his or her most gut-wrenching memory. I lay in bed with my husband, watching television, completely taking for granted the hundreds of times I'd lounged like that before without incident. The ribbed, long-sleeve shirt I was wearing over my pajama bottoms was hiking up a little on me, and as I adjusted it my hand brushed against the side of my body. It was a moment I realized that something wasn't right, something didn't feel right. The only thing "right" was where the swelling was, on the far right-hand side of my breast.

Wait, I thought. *It must be my bra.*

Wait, I thought again. *I'm not wearing a bra. In fact, I don't own a bra.*

More desperate grasping followed. *OK. Then it must be my shirt. My thick shirt. Some kind of bump in my thick shirt. No. The shirt I'm wearing is a very thin material.* I was running out of sanity-preserving ideas.

My body shot straight up like a launched rocket. What I was feeling… was *me*. My skin. My swelling. A swelling that… to the best of my knowledge… had no business being where it was.

I had my husband, a pediatrician, feel it.

"Oh," he said, reassuringly. "That feels like a fibroid cyst. I just saw a girl in my office last week with the same thing."

"Just like this?" I asked. I was panting like a dog at a treat.

"Yep."

So that was it. I believed him. But… I'd still need to get it checked. Just to make sure. Right?

I slowly lay back down again. Someone said something on the television, but I really couldn't hear what it was. I could only hear the thoughts in my head.

I'd just make sure.

Tomorrow.

I called the local Harvard Vanguard the following morning. An appointment was scheduled for me for later that afternoon, which I was thankful for but at the same time frankly wishing it hadn't been treated with such urgency. If I'd told them I had an ingrown toenail, would they have similarly taken me in on the same day? Or a pustulating boil? Or an anal fistula that would put King Louis XIV to shame? What did it take to be hustled in like that? Was it just slow there and they happened to have a vacancy that on a busier day they wouldn't have? Was I thinking too much?

My blood pressure was taken first. It was high. My weight was measured next with all of my clothes- and heavy boots- on. It was needling me that this information, skewed and weird, especially the high blood pressure reading as it had always been low in previous checkups, was going to be funneled to the physician that was going to see me and give me my first assessment of what was going on.

When I saw the doctor, a middle-aged Asian woman, she seemed kind-hearted and jovial, with enough smiles and chuckling during our little stretch of small talk to put me initially at ease. Then we got down to business.

"Do you have a family history of breast cancer?" she asked.

"Yes. My mother was diagnosed with breast cancer. It was stage IV," I said. "It had spread to her lungs."

"How old was she?"

I tried to remember her exact age at diagnosis. "It was in her late 60's."

The doctor nodded and wrote something down. She soon started examining the mass by just pressing down on it and crudely measuring its circumference with her fingertips, and I naively confided in her what my husband had said about it feeling like a benign fibroid cyst. It was then that her sense of humor really kicked in, and after a snort and chortle that was dripping with condescension, she told me that you can't tell by just feeling it what it is. And then she said, "It's too firm to be a cyst." *But... didn't she... just... tell me that you can't tell... Ah, never mind.*

The doctor then told me that she would order a mammography and ultrasound, and she would try to get this for me in a week. My first thought was, a week? I was hustled in here within 24 hours based on a flimsy over the phone description of who knows what, but now that it's been sized up as "too firm to be a cyst" by a credentialed professional, I may or may not be scheduled to come in again for up to seven whole days? I knew enough from my own experience and training in cancer research that biologically, at this unknown stage, a few days might not really make all that much of a difference. But *psychologically*, every passing day that was not focused on the problem at hand felt like eternity.

A nurse who had been standing at the reception desk and listening in on our conversation waited quietly for the doctor to leave. She then said to me in a low, reassuring tone, "They will probably be able to get you an appointment in a couple of days. The radiology staff shouldn't be too busy."

I waited to be called.

But there was no call.

It was a day later, and at the very least I wanted to know when the mammography and ultrasound would be scheduled. If I had to wait a whole week, I'd make sure to stock up on hard liquor. If I was going to be taken care of immediately, I would give my liver a break.

So instead of staring at the phone and trying to use my psychic energies to get it to ring, I called them instead, only to find out the inexplicable, damning truth that the doctor hadn't ordered me anything. Seriously? This was a true "what the f???" moment that forced me to use as much restraint as I could to not try to physically reach through the wires and punch the person on the other end. What kept the scene from turning ugly was that intuitively I knew the receptionist I was talking to was not the problem. I knew that it was my laugh riot stand up comedian of a physician that had dropped the ball and hung me out to dry for reasons that went beyond my comprehension. This was, after all, kind of an urgent matter, wasn't it?

"Uh... Why..." I stammered. "Why wasn't an appointment set up?"

There was an echo of dumbfounded stammering on the other end. "I'm not sure," the receptionist said. "Let me see what we have available." There were a few seconds of silence before she said, "So it looks like the earliest appointment I can get for you is in... two weeks."

You have to be kidding. "But... A nurse told me I'd probably be able to get something in just a couple of days."

"Oh, no," the receptionist said. "I don't know who told you that. We're booked."

"Okay." I hung up the phone, defeated. I tried to think of where the nearest liquor store was.

The nurse/receptionist, whose name I learned was Lisa, called me back. "We can do better," she said. "I have an opening one week from now."

"Thanks," I said, my tone softer, but the dejection in my voice still irrepressible. "I appreciate you calling me back and trying to get me in sooner."

She called me back a *third* time and said, "Guess what. We're in luck. I just got a cancellation for tomorrow."

I was grateful for her caring and persistence, and I thanked her, this woman named Lisa that I'd forever remember as my angel from the heavens above. The image I had of myself buying a week's worth of booze to drown my sorrows in was quickly replaced by an image of myself buying an evening's worth of celebratory champagne. I was going to get some answers. And I wasn't going to have to wait a week or longer to get them.

Or so I thought.

Lisa knew who I was as soon as I approached the front desk of the radiology department. I resisted the urge to hug her and made a bee line for my mammography, where

I could look forward to having my right breast squashed flat like a marshmallow in a smore.

The technician was blond and perky, and seemingly hell-bent on removing the panic that was obviously plastered on my face.

"You look nervous," she said. Her words reminded me of my very first mammography, when my mother's battle with metastatic, hormone-responsive breast cancer was in its infancy and I was hyperemotional and had unexpectedly broken down in tears. I kept it together during all of the mammograms that followed, but my mother was very much on mind during each and every one.

She motioned for me to take a look at an image she had taken. "To me, this looks just like a cyst. See how perfectly round it is?" I had to squint to see what she was referring to, this faint outline of a circle in the midst of a gray and black pixelated mess. It reminded me of the worst of the protein gels I'd run during the years in the lab, probed with a really, really crappy antibody with an unacceptably high noise:signal ratio. Such a result would be considered unable to be easily interpreted and not of publication quality.

I was looking at what would be described to me later as "dense breast tissue," which is difficult to see beyond. Even the questionable ball of flesh that was big enough to be palpable and detected by me just sweeping my pointer finger past it was barely visible on the screen to the naked eye in the midst of all that opaqueness.

I had an ultrasound, or sonography, next. It was a fair alternative to the mammogram, with sound waves being used to "read" the strange swelling inside of me. The ultrasound technician was just as bubbly and friendly as the mammography technician and had put me completely at ease with lots of smiles and small talk. She left the room to consult with the radiologist, and I readied myself for both of them to walk back in and tell me the swelling was just as the mammography technician had said: no biggie, just a cyst.

While I waited for them, I started making a mental list of all of the dietary changes I would be making to be healthier, having been given this stern warning and second chance. I was in the middle of planning to switch some of my coffee consumption to green and black tea, to eat more fish and resist the temptation to get the convenient drive-thru Happy Meals on my commute home from work in the evenings, when the Grim Reaper walked through the door disguised as a radiologist with wispy, longish gray hair cradling the top of a high forehead and a deceptive twinkle in his eye.

He smiled and shook my hand. Some pleasantries were exchanged.

"What do you do?" he asked.

Lately? Worry, I thought. "I do leukemia research," I said.

"So, you're a doctor?" he asked.

"A researcher," I said. "I have my Ph.D. in pharmacology."

The pleasantries abruptly ended.

"According to the ultrasound, what you have is definitely not a cyst," he said. "As it's abnormal tissue, you will need a biopsy."

Not the result I was expecting. I attempted the same joke I'd been saying to anyone who would listen for the past couple of days. "I'm too busy for this," and "I'm sorry, but my schedule just doesn't easily accommodate being sick."

The joke did not go over well with the Grim Reaper, who quipped, "I'm sure a lot of people could say the same thing."

No, I thought. *I was just joking. Swear. Promise.* I didn't genuinely think that I was so special that I should be separated from the masses and exonerated from illness just because I was a cancer researcher and mother with time-consuming hobbies and parents with major health issues I needed to help support and I barely had enough time as a reasonably healthy person to keep all of that in motion. I was just sayin'...

The Grim Reaper told me that 75 to 80% of biopsies turn out to be nothing, and that the odds were in my favor. Then he added, "I realize for you it's going to be either 0 or 100%."

Such a funny guy.

I made the mistake of trying to pry information out of him that I hoped would make me feel better. I thought back to the mammography and the perfect circle the bubbly technician had pointed out amidst the blurry gray background. "But it's fairly isolated, right?" I asked.

The Grim Reaper shook his head and said in a non-committal tone, "Now we can't say anything based on the ultrasound. We have to wait for the results of the biopsy."

More waiting.

Yay.

My husband and daughter and I went to a chain restaurant that evening for dinner. I picked at my meal. This did not seem to be a time for enjoyment of life or its celebration. Instead, it was a somber reminder of the sudden twists and turns life could take at any moment, especially when we are least expecting it.

Part 2

A biopsy was scheduled, a whopping ten days from my mammogram and ultrasound Danse Macabre with Dr. Twinkle-In-His-Eye. Until that day came, I made sure to continue moving along as usual, keeping my nose to the proverbial grindstone, and respecting any and all prearranged meetings with colleagues. Any desire I may have had to curl up in a tiny ball at the edge of my bed and stare blankly for hours on end at cracks in the wall or wayward flying insects would have to be tempered by the reality that time was not going to stand still for me.

My first meeting was in the tiny, paper strewn office of a colleague at the cancer center where I worked, a hematologist-oncologist and long-term collaborator. He had been a co-advisor and author on a number of published papers over the years, and at the time of our meeting he had just finished conducting a clinical trial that was bringing a leukemia drug I had identified in a screen very close to FDA approval. Several years earlier, he had also been instrumental in helping me get a second opinion on scans of my mother's lungs that showed possible metastasis of her breast cancer to their periphery. I never would have predicted back then that I'd be seeking yet more support from him years later, for myself.

"So how are you?" he asked.

Little did he know what a loaded question that would be, and how much it would delay us from discussing the new data I'd generated. I told him that I was going through something a little unnerving, that abnormal tissue was detected in my right breast and I was scheduled for a biopsy in ten days.

"I can help you set up an appointment here if you want," he said. He was referring to our beloved Dana-Farber Cancer Institute.

I smiled and thanked him, but shook my head. At that point, I wanted to keep fully alive and kicking the possibility of the mass being benign.

Making an appointment at the cancer hospital where I worked felt like too much, too soon, and I opted instead to sweat out the week and a half and keep my humble appointment at the quiet and unassuming northern Massachusetts-based Harvard Vanguard.

Despite my really not wanting the conversation to get yet more personal, the pros and cons of the size and density of my breasts were raised, as was the fact that I was an Ashkenazi Jew, with a higher prevalence of the BRCA breast cancer gene in that population. The darkness of the conversation was brightened by the reality of the statistics, with up to eighty percent of growths in the breasts turning out to be non-malignant. Right?

I worked over the next ten days, and I played. I celebrated the fiftieth birthday of a friend of mine, a musician, who was singing at a restaurant in a nearby town. I had a photo taken with a mutual friend of ours, in front of a large window that bordered the outside sidewalk. There was a glare that was making it difficult to get the picture taken without the two of us looking washed out. I found the light to be symbolic, as I was trying very hard to be there, but in reality I was only there to an extent.

On the day of the procedure, which was an ultrasound-guided biopsy, I was nervous, nervous to the point of my whole body physically shaking. I didn't understand where all the vibration was coming from and what subconscious fears and worries were going on to cause all that crazy ruckus inside of me. I had no idea if the biopsy would be painful or painless, if it would tickle or sting, if it would send me into a deep, dark depression or make me deliriously show tune-singing happy. What I did know was that pieces of this strange growth in my breast were going to be removed and analyzed and the result was either going to be something or nothing. And I supposed that knowledge was enough to make me tremble uncontrollably.

A nurse standing near my bed, who saw all of my weird tics and convulsions, asked if I was cold and needed a blanket. I tried explaining that I really didn't think I was feeling chilled, but rather that I just wasn't good with medical techniques. I also genuinely and sincerely wished I could be just about anywhere else than in that room with her waiting for a portion of my body to be excised and examined, but I didn't tell her that.

My biggest concern was whether the doctor doing the biopsy would have a better sense of humor than Dr. Twinkle-In-His-Eye. As he was preparing instruments for the procedure, he asked me what I did for a living. My nervous shaking became nervous chattering as I blabbed on about how I did cancer research and how we were working on drugs that affect that intracellular machinery to promote selective and targeted degradation of cancer-causing proteins. Blah, blah, teeth chattering, blah.

Pleasantries were exchanged, but this time with no sudden startling revelations that made me feel sucker-punched. That was because any results I'd be getting from this round of testing I was told would be on a different day and not by any member of this medical team. I learned that the radiologist, like me, was also Jewish and I quipped about him being a "member of the tribe." There was some laughter, and a few more inane back and forth comments that were helping to calm my nerves.

I threw a few names at him of people I worked with, and he humored me by agreeing the names rang a bell. I was on a roll. This had been really starting to work to distract me from the nauseating thought of what was yet to come. I continued to try to come up with physicians or researchers that I knew in my heart he probably had never heard of, when he abruptly changed the subject to the task at hand.

"So we can't talk shop anymore?" I asked, making sure to sound dejected.

"No, sorry," he said. "We need to get started."

The last thing I wanted to do was disrupt his concentration, should it be commensurate with failed attempts and the need to repeat digging into me to get what he needed. I quickly sobered up by thinking gloomy thoughts, which at that moment, unfortunately, really wasn't all that difficult to do.

"Do you want to watch the screen?" he asked. What he meant was, did I want to watch weird images that would have to be explained to me on the screen of the ultrasound while they chipped away at my insides.

Do you want to watch me projectile vomit? I thought. I politely said, "no" and turned my head almost as far as Linda Blair's head turned in the Exorcist, which had not so surprisingly come to mind.

Nine excruciatingly painful and loud snipping sensations later, I was lamenting having not asked for more anesthetic. I felt more than what I'd hoped I'd be feeling as they took their samples of whatever this as-of-yet unnamed thing was inside of me. But since it was more of an achiness than a sharp, stabbing pain, I decided not to be a big whiny crybaby and take it like a man. A man that- considering what I was going through- I secretly wished I was. I would only learn later that numbing the crap out of oneself was key to a painless biopsy.

What was more unsettling than the procedure itself was this ice-cold pack they slapped on the area that was biopsied. They told me to hold it in place for a while, but as it was only literally adding insult to injury, I only pretended to hold it against me for any length of time. I was escorted by a nurse to another room to have the epitome of oxymorons they described as a "gentle mammography" done so that they could get an image of a chip they had placed inside of the growth. The same technician who had done the original mammography was waiting for me. She had been the one that tried to calm my nerves by attempting to convince me that the growth looked to her like it was just a cyst. I wondered what she was thinking as I entered the room after being biopsied, with her gaze slightly averted, a sad but possibly pitying smile on her face.

Despite all the pressure I'd put on the biopsied area with ice, there was a lot of bleeding, which the mammography technician didn't seem to be expecting as she hastily ran out of the room to fetch gauze. There was a box of tissues on the counter next to where I was sitting. I just pulled one out and dabbed at the blood, not giving much thought at the time to the potential significance of it. Tumors encapsulate themselves in blood vessels.

The technician returned with a fistful of gauze, but by then I was proudly surveying the successful job the Kleenex and my thumb had done. She had tried positioning me to get an image of the clip, but it was to no avail. It was too deep to be easily seen by mammography. As the ultrasound had detected the clip earlier, it was decided that the additional imaging by mammography was unnecessary.

I was relieved of further senseless irradiation and discomfort and sent home. I rested for a couple of hours in bed, a partially melted ice pack in place. I had work I needed to do in the lab, and so I drove there to get it done. I found myself wincing every so often while I pipetted leukemia cells into tiny wells in a microtiter plate, thinking about what I'd been through. The snapping sound. The pain. The ice. The bleeding.

Three days later, my husband and I went to the scheduled office appointment to get the results of the biopsy. I was once again weighed with my boots and all of my clothes on, and my blood pressure was checked and was- yet again- high. As we waited in an office for my primary care physician that someone randomly designated to me and whom I'd never met before, I can't say that I felt overly worried or concerned. In retrospect, that was undoubtedly a mistake. I had found more often than not over the years that a dollop of pessimism, sprinkled with a pinch of hysteria, for some reason helped ward off bad things. It's almost as though this kind of thinking strips the Powers That Be of the ability to shock and rattle and they just give up since there's no fun in it anymore. My whole life, I'd been half-jokingly referred to by friends as a complete neurotic, but what they didn't realize was how being a neurotic was my modus operandi for survival.

So, I sat in a chair next to my husband, assuming what I had was indeed one of those hormonally-induced, benign fibroadenomas I'd read about, which could range anywhere between the size of a pea and a golf ball. A golf ball! I couldn't even imagine having something that huge inside of me that's just a big lump of nothing that isn't going to go anywhere. And what I had seemed roughly to be about the size of a small marble. To fuel my wishful thinking even more was the fact that I was premenopausal at the time of the mammography and ultrasound. Bang! Obviously, there were oodles of up to no good hormones flying devilishly around inside of me, giving me these weird feverish sensations in the chest area every month and making odd things happen and strange growths pop up out of nowhere. Add to the mix the fact that I'd turned 50 earlier in the year, the age at which folks are strongly encouraged to have polyps checked in the back end and women are slated to start going through menopause if it hadn't happened already. *Of course* I was destined to experience this plethora of oddities, and I was convinced that what I had was just this goofy, harmless mass of misplaced flesh that arose from my body's biological clock having ticked as much as it was ever going to.

The primary care physician walked in and shook my hand and my husband's. She didn't look particularly happy, which my husband pointed out later as having been the moment that he "knew." The words, "Your biopsy came back positive for invasive ductal carcinoma," were uttered from the primary care physician's taut lips, and there was no pause or breath taken before she followed up with, "Would you like for me to write you a prescription for Ativan?" It had become obvious to me at that moment that the Grim Reaper had returned in a more feminine and expectedly humorless form. And if I had been raised in a rainforest by monkeys and had known absolutely nothing about cancer, her offer of a lorazepam script would have told me in no uncertain terms that what I had was something really, really bad.

I have to drive by the Harvard Vanguard building every day as part of my commute to and from work. The building always summons a memory of my husband, standing outside it and facing me after we were given the diagnosis. I suppose it's natural when the question of one's mortality is touched on for the philosopher residing deep within to be wooed out of hiding. I found myself suddenly reflecting on how good or bad life had been or how good or bad I had been, and if things could have been better or different or if things needed to start being better or different.

"Would you be happier without me?" I asked.

A pause, the "You're being ridiculous" facial expression, and "Of course not. What are you talking about?"

"You love me?"

"Yes."

A hug, a kiss, the wind blowing through our hair on that cool, March day.

Part 3

I was scheduled to meet next with a surgeon through Harvard Vanguard. He had dark features and an accent I couldn't place and was a hell of a nice guy. Despite claiming to be suffering from a migraine, he smiled and was pleasant and guaranteed me another 50 years of life, although he said he couldn't promise me more than that. He told me that I had what he referred to as the "garden-variety type of breast cancer." Estrogen receptor- and progesterone receptor-rich, hormone-responsive, HER2-negative. I knew the phrasing was meant to be heartening, but it was not by any stretch of the imagination the kind of fruits and vegetables I'd ever have selected to be growing in my backyard.

He explained the basics of breast cancer and how it makes a pit stop in sentinel lymph nodes before characteristically carrying on its mission elsewhere in the body. The sentinel lymph nodes would be removed and tested for the presence of cancer at the time of surgery. He had suggested genetic testing to see if I was positive for the BRCA gene, which would change the course of treatment as BRCA positivity carries a very high risk of ovarian and breast cancer and double mastectomy and removal of the ovaries would be strongly encouraged. However, he suggested I get an MRI to examine the lymph nodes and get a better idea of how localized the tumor was. He felt underneath my arms and said he didn't feel any enlarged lymph nodes.

I had been encouraged by some friends and family to get treatment at the cancer hospital I worked at in Boston, mainly because of the convenience of being able to transition easily from work to appointments. The time had come for me to take my collaborator from the tiny paper-strewn office up on his offer and accept the fact that I was now eligible to be a cancer patient at the hospital where I'd studiously and mechanically manipulated the peripheral blood and bone marrow cells of leukemia patients for over two decades.

I felt a bit deceptive sitting in this kind surgeon's office and listening as he pushed through the discomfort of his migraine and continued discussing plans for my treatment. Luckily, he was the one, as opposed to me, who brought up the fact that often patients will opt to get a second opinion as well as treatment in Boston. He said that I could do the same, however he insisted that I would be told the exact same thing he was telling me. I sheepishly admitted that I was considering treatment where I worked, but only because of the convenience of it. He seemed to understand.

Before leaving the building, I told my husband I wanted to see Lisa, the nurse/receptionist, in radiology. Another nurse at the main desk tracked her down for me, and when she saw me she immediately motioned for me to follow her through the door behind the front desk for privacy. I told her about my diagnosis, and she thanked me for letting her know, claiming that nurses are forbidden from following up on certain patients on their own. She gave me some words of encouragement, and then she hugged me. She was a stranger who helped me more than she would ever know, a stranger who I would likely never see again, but someone I would never forget.

The real fun began at the Dana-Farber Cancer Institute, on the ninth floor of a building adjacent to the facility where I had been doing my leukemia research. My first meeting was with a red-haired oncologist whose face was familiar to me, likely from seeing articles written about her many achievements that were published in the hospital's monthly newsletter. She was accompanied by a very young-looking, dark-haired male assistant, a medical fellow. He was given the privilege of watching all of the color drain from my face as the oncologist said "Wait, hold on... What's this?" while digging her fingers painfully deeply into my right arm pit. It was my second time lying on my back on the examining table like a slab of meat being tenderized. The medical fellow had fished around, as well, only moments earlier, and like the kind surgeon who had initially seen me and would never see me again, he didn't feel anything enlarged or otherwise out of the ordinary.

I slowly sat up after the last of the digging into my armpit was over and pulled the rose-colored johnny back over my shoulder. My eyes followed the oncologist as she took a few steps away from the examining table.

"I'm sorry." Her eyes locked with mine. "I have to tell you," she said with a shrug, as though she felt some kind of justification for giving it to me straight was warranted.

It was not a good day for me to be receiving news. The oncologist explained to me that, in addition to having at least one lymph node suspiciously enlarged and possibly positive for the presence of cancer, the estimated size of the lump in my breast was such that a simple, tissue-conserving lumpectomy would not be possible. She was pretty confident that the surgeon, whom I was scheduled to meet with the following day, would be in favor of shrinking the tumor first with medicine and then performing a much simpler, less invasive surgery. One option offered to me was enrolling in a clinical trial and being simultaneously treated with Lupron, which shuts off estrogen production from the ovaries, and tamoxifen, which blocks estrogen from acting on estrogen receptors. Both would be recommended to me as I was premenopausal at the time of diagnosis and shutting down estrogen production and blocking estrogen activity would be expected to help starve my hormone-responsive cancer and prevent it from growing. Depending on which arm of the study I would be randomly selected for, it was possible that I would also receive a third drug called palbociclib, which blocks a protein involved in cell division and was already FDA-approved for metastatic breast cancer in postmenopausal women.

There was a little naive fantasy that had been incubating in my mind, in which the cancer would be plucked out of me, lickety-split, and I would be on my merry way with life resuming as I once knew it, and all would be well once again in my world. My reality was suddenly looking like I would be walking around for six months with a cancerous mass in my right breast that would hopefully diminish in size with daily consumption of tamoxifen and palbociclib tablets and a once a month shot in the butt with Lupron, followed by surgery and radiation and a big question mark as to whether there would be additional treatments- including chemotherapy.

Alas, this nightmare was not going to go away anytime soon.

The surgeon met with me briefly, mild-mannered with big brown eyes and a gentle smile. I heard a chorus of angels singing and basked happily in a glow of light emanating from his head as he reassured me that, in contrast to what the oncologist believed, he didn't see anything in the lymph node realm that looked suspicious, according to my scans, and that it was common for there to be reactionary enlargement of the lymph nodes following a biopsy. *Ah hah*! I thought. *Oncologist wrong. Surgeon right.*

I silently nodded in agreement with my overly simplistic, black and white thinking. Or, more accurately, I silently nodded in agreement with my overly simplistic *wishful* thinking. Rational thought barged its way in just then and reminded me that just because I wanted something to be a certain way didn't mean it really was that way, and of the two opposing views one was correct, and only more tests would eventually reveal the truth.

The surgeon gave me more or less the same breast cancer 101 refresher course that the first surgeon had given me. Knowing the oncologist had informed me about the clinical trial the day before, and perhaps to confuse me more and make it impossible for me to ever reach a decision as to what to do, he explained that studies suggested life expectancy was the same regardless of whether pre-op drug treatment was done first, or surgery was done first. He said that he could perform the surgery at any time but considering the size of the tumor it would be aesthetically challenging.

The part of me that just wanted the cancer removed from my body took over then and I found myself saying, "I really don't care about things like that, what it'll look like. It's not like I'm a Playboy Bunny or member of a nudist colony."

His response was, with what I was realizing was his trademark, kind smile, "Then I'll care about that for you."

Despite having made the choice to stay in school through my mid 20's, I always hated tests. I never minded studying for them, and even for the most part tolerated taking them, but I had a really strong distaste for the piercing anxiety that always came with finding out how well or poorly I did on them. The first stretch of several weeks post diagnosis were riddled with tests, carrying with them the same heart-thumping anticipation I used to experience in my school days. Except there were no "A's", "B's", or "C's" waiting for me at the end of this round of exams. And this frankly made me wistful for my old test-taking days.

The very first on the list of scheduled examinations I had to get was genetic testing, to determine if I had the BRCA gene, or any other known familial cancer-causing gene that might shed some light on what I had as well as what I might be at increased risk of getting in the future. In response to the geneticist's request for me to allow her to draw blood from my arm for this, I asked if there was another less invasive option, like a saliva swab or something. I had no idea at the time how numb and desensitized I would become to the fear of having needles pierce my skin and things being injected into me or sucked out of me, as I slipped into the role of human pin cushion for the next twelve months. But that day, the geneticist humored me, despite claiming to never before have used the plastic collection tube that I squeezed a Q-tip into over and over again that had repeatedly been pressed against my gums. Amazingly, and disgustingly, the cotton captured enough saliva from my mouth to fill up two tubes and bring me closer to discovering the truth about my gene pool.

An e-mail from the geneticist delivered the good news that I was BRCA negative and the even better news that I was negative for anything and everything else on the list of unfriendly genes that I was being tested for. There was an article that I'd read recently in mainstream news about 72 new genetic mutations linked to breast cancer that had been discovered. The fact that I shared with my mother the same disease in the same subcategory, and so many cousins on my father's side were breast cancer survivors, still seemed to me to smack of something that might be inherited, possibly falling into the as-of-yet undiscovered subset of genes behaving badly.

But the culprit similarly could be a shared penchant for artificially colored red, yellow and blue dye-laden rainbow ice cream cakes decorated with maraschino cherries or hanging out too close to the microwave while waiting for hotdogs to heat up, or even just eating the hotdogs themselves. As it was impossible to say with any confidence what the real root of all evils was for me and my family, as well as whether it was one root or many roots and if the roots were inside or outside the body, I took solace in the fact that the genetic testing I had was negative for the list of aberrant genes I had been tested for, including BRCA.

It was simply one less thing that I had to worry about.

The next test on my list was magnetic resonance imaging (or MRI), which was to be focused on my chest and used to reveal, as the very first surgeon I'd met with had explained, how localized the tumor was in the right breast. In retrospect, I suppose my fear of the MRI illuminating disseminated cancer in my chest like a Lite-Brite toy was a little irrational. But the cancer diagnosis in and of itself was frankly enough to put my mind in a very dark place, and this pessimism was what I found myself to be continually working against.

An IV was put into my hand before the MRI for contrast dye to be infused. There was something both perverse and invigorating about visiting my lab right after this and finishing an experiment in this condition. It was a multi-tasking of sorts, I supposed, in an unsettling, disturbing kind of way.

I carefully timed my experiment to finish with just enough minutes left over to get to the MRI on time. As I funneled through the machine, face down, the image of a person being buried alive came to mind. I was asked if I wanted music to play through the headphones they had placed on me. I said "yes" and when asked what kind of music I wanted, I said "classic rock." I could just barely hear probably the worst three or four songs ever made by Led Zeppelin and AC/DC. The songs were so bad that I found myself relieved to have them muffled by the knocking and thumping sounds of the MRI. The contrast dye felt cold as it was pumped through my vessels, and a bizarre taste and smell that I can only describe as nothing that a human being should be subjected to tasting and smelling quickly followed to add a touch of yet more surrealism to my day.

The medical fellow told me the results of the MRI over the phone. There was good news, in that there was nothing looking out of whack on my left side, which meant the action was confined to my right side. But... the MRI confirmed that the action on the right side was a bit out of control. That one lymph node the oncologist suspected was enlarged was indeed... boastfully prideful and full of itself. It was still unknown at this point whether the lymph node was larger than it should have been because it was stuffed like a Thanksgiving turkey with cancer cells or if it was, as my kind and gentle surgeon suggested, inflamed from that one horrendous and painful biopsy. But regardless of whether the lymph node wore a black cowboy hat or a white one, its puffy presence was intimidating, and somebody had to take that bastard down.

There was just one more test that I had to have, which was a consequence of my having high enough bilirubin levels to possibly disqualify me for the clinical trial. I was scheduled for an ultrasound of my liver to make sure there were no obstructions there. At this point, I wasn't sure if I could handle anymore news of something being discovered in my body that shouldn't be there. But it didn't seem that I was given any choice but to endure yet another deep sea diving expedition in my internal organs.

Part 4: Conclusion

When I walked into the room where the ultrasound was to be performed, I was greeted by an older gentleman (the ultrasound technician), as well as two younger men in black suits and ties, whom I gathered- based on their interactions with the technician- were not in fact Blues Brothers impersonators but may instead have been representatives of the company the ultrasound equipment was purchased through.

Three strange men.

One me, feeling strangely exposed in front of three strange men.

As politely as I could, I asked if all three of them had to stay in the room as the technician lifted my shirt up and pulled my pants partway down to get access to my liver and gallbladder and whatever else was in the vicinity. Both of the men in suits were very nice and accommodating. One obliged by leaving the room to grab a cup of coffee.

I wrestled a bit with the technician who continued to try to raise my shirt and keep my pants down at a certain level.

"Do you not want to have this procedure?" he asked in a gentle, even tone.

"I do," I lied, loosening my grip on my clothes and waving the white flag of surrender. I held my breath every time he hovered over an area with the ultrasound probe and kept moving it back and forth over and over again and looking at the screen.

"Do you see anything?" I asked. "Is there anything there? In my liver? Gallbladder? Pancreas?" *Is there another tumor? Is there more than one? Is it something other than a tumor? Am I about to give birth any second to an alien baby like in Village of the Damned?*

The technician told me to take some deep breaths and kept probing and analyzing the screen. After what seemed like hours, but was probably more like 20 minutes or so, the ultrasound probe was retired, and I was able to cover my midriff again.

A doctor visited me afterward and told me that my liver, pancreas and gallbladder were fine. I had to restrain myself from jumping for joy at the news that I had at least three body parts that were not disfigured or diseased. I thanked the technician for doing such a good job and helping me to get some decent news for a change. He told me he must be my good luck charm. He also lied to me and told me I was an "excellent patient." I knew I sucked, but it was nice of him to try to make me think he thought otherwise.

"You have a bit more tumor burden there than we'd like to see," said the medical fellow.

"We are trying to make it so that you will never have to come back here and see us again," said the oncologist.

"We are trying to avoid having you need to take Adriamycin or some other hard-hitting chemotherapy," said both the oncologist and the medical fellow.

It was settled. I'd opt to be enrolled in the clinical trial that, through a six-month pre-op combination of hormone therapy and palbociclib, would attempt to shrink the tumor to a size that would allow for a simple lumpectomy and at the same time maybe... just *maybe*... nail anything that might have ventured out of the questionable lymph node to distal parts of my body. The big bummer for me was the need for two biopsies to be carried out in the first few weeks of the trial, as I was suffering from serious post-traumatic stress disorder from the first one that left me bruised and in pain for weeks. The biopsies alone were almost a deal breaker for me, but the arguments presented in favor of the trial and the long-term potential benefits to be gained were enough to get me to buck up and put on my big girl panties.

As I lay on the table in the room where the first of the two biopsies was to be performed, it occurred to me the number of people between hospitals I'd been at that had seen me shirtless. Me, the kind of person who feels embarrassed taking my clothes off in a dressing room in front of one of those big mirrors that may or may not be accompanied by a surveillance camera. My mother told me that after a while, you bear yourself so often that it doesn't faze you anymore. I wondered how long it would take me to reach that point.

A fine needle aspiration of the suspicious-looking lymph node was performed as part of the first biopsy to be the tie-breaker between the two opposing predictions of why it was enlarged. I felt far less pain during this procedure than I had for the very first, horrifying one because they made sure to numb the hell out of me this time around. For the next and final biopsy that followed, I was numbed up even more, to the point where my breasts could have been replaced by bowling balls right then and there and I doubt I would have felt the slightest twinge.

The pain that I did feel on both biopsy days was more of an emotional one, a realization as I looked at the "MRN" patient code typed on my paper bracelet that I was on the other side of where I'd been for years. I always had acknowledged that there were real people behind the countless "MRN" patient codes that I'd seen typed on the labels on heparin-coated tubes of blood from leukemia patients. I'd read the names and genders and ages and I'd often form an image in my mind of what they might look like. But there was a kind of detached indifference when I did this, as though my science-oriented brain, just to be able to get the job done, had insulated and protected itself from the distraction of feeling any kind of emotion.

Now, I was an "MRN" number, my name, age and gender typed on the labels of heparin-coated tubes of blood passed along to Institute staff members performing analyses as part of the clinical trial I was enrolled in. I wondered what was going through their own science-oriented minds as they read the labels and went about doing their jobs.

A clinical trial nurse came into the room to collect samples following the second biopsy.

"Will this biopsy tell us if the drugs are working?" I asked her.

"We won't know until the end of the study," she said, which was six months away. "Some patients ask to have an ultrasound midway through to determine which way the tumor is going. You may want to ask your oncologist."

"Yes," I said. "I'm planning on that. She had told me that at a certain point in time, if the drugs are not effective, we'd move to plan B."

She nodded.

"My problem," I continued, "is that the main focus of my research is trying to understand and overcome mechanisms of drug resistance. What I've been doing for a living is always on my mind, and it makes it hard. I'd like to know while the cancer is in me that the medications that I'm taking are battling it."

One physician who had remained in the room as I was uncontrollably neurotic said she completely understood.

"I do a lot of synergy studies," I said. "And I've read very good things about palbociclib, and I know theoretically my tumor- which is 95% progesterone and estrogen receptor-positive- should respond to the tamoxifen and Lupron. It's just so surreal for me to go from hoping drug combination treatments work for the purpose of getting a publication or a grant, to hoping they work for my *life*."

I received a look of sympathy from the remaining physician. One of several I'd received since I got on my soapbox.

I was sitting at my desk at home when I received a call from the medical fellow, who first congratulated me on the FDA approval of the anti-leukemia drug I had identified in a drug screen. The initial euphoric high he put me on, though, was sliced to pieces around thirty seconds later, when he told me the fine needle biopsy had confirmed the presence of cancer in the one enlarged sentinel lymph node.

Even though I admittedly suspected it, I was still oddly numb.

The next six months of daily pill popping and monthly shots in the rear end while knowingly carting around a malignant mass and at least one contaminated lymph node went by surprisingly fast. The hormone therapy had pushed me into an early menopause, and I found myself often oscillating many times a day between feeling like I was in the Arctic tundra and feeling like I was in a sauna, and the palbociclib occasionally lowered my white blood cell counts and I'd need to stop taking it prematurely to allow the counts to recover before resuming treatment again.

I palpated the mass every so often and generally didn't feel much change until several months into the treatment. To my delight and surprise and utter relief, I found myself having to go searching for the same lump that had been prominent enough to send me into a frenzied, hysterical panic on that one fateful television watching evening.

Rough measurements were taken by several of the medical staff and were compared with the original measurements taken six months prior. The tumor mass was believed to have shrunk to approximately one-eighth of its original size, and the enlarged lymph node was also believed to have diminished in size.

"This bodes well for the clinical trial," I excitedly said to one of the clinical trial nurses, unable to suppress the quaver in my voice.

"This bodes well for your *life*," she said, pointedly, momentarily snapping me out of what I can only describe as having been in this bizarre super nerd researcher mode. How I could have, for that moment, placed progression of science as a priority over my own mortality I'm not sure. But I did.

Just when I thought that all of the nerve-wracking evaluations and measurements and grading were finished, the medical fellow told me that they needed to perform an "Oncotype DX," which measured levels of 21 breast cancer genes to establish a score that would tell them if my cancer was aggressive and at a high risk for recurrence. A low score meant the cancer had a low risk, whereas a high score meant that there was a high risk, and the benefit of treatment with standard chemotherapy, like "The Red Devil" or Adriamycin (doxorubicin), outweighed the cost of the drug's nasty side effects.

The medical fellow called. I hesitated picking the phone up for a moment and braced myself, the harrowing theme of lymph node positivity during our last over-the-phone conversation at the forefront of my mind. He promptly told me that the oncotype score came back and it was a "9," which was low. It indicated that I wouldn't benefit from chemotherapy. So the plan of action for me was... surgery followed by radiation followed by several years of hormone therapy and a biannual intravenous infusion of a bone strengthening drug that also prevents metastasis.

Surgery was scheduled, on my birthday of all days, which I must admit I did not even try to keep a secret from the medical staff. I happily basked in many parties of pity thrown for me from the presurgery room to when I was pushed in a wheelchair to be picked up outside the hospital. Because of the anesthesia, my only memories of the event were being taken on a gurney into the surgery room one moment, and then waking up, babbling incoherently about lord knows what to a nurse who was blatantly ignoring everything I was saying the next. I had a feeling she was used to that sort of thing.

The sentinel lymph node that had originally tested positive for cancer was tested again after it was surgically removed. When the medical fellow called me to tell me whether the excised lymph node had residual cancer, I figured based on the mixed bag of both good and bad news he had given to me in our past phone conversations it could go either way this time. Alas the verdict was not uplifting. I was encouraged to have a second surgery that would remove axillary lymph nodes that would similarly be tested for the presence of cancer. If positive, I was told the game plan would change and I'd likely be put on chemotherapy. If negative, I could jump for joy, but only after I'd healed sufficiently to be able to do so.

The next surgery was around two weeks later. I found myself looking forward to being zonked out again on anesthesia and having the experience of not remembering a damn thing between the moments before and after surgery and spewing stream of consciousness musings out to whoever was closest to where I was recovering.

The pain I felt this time, post-surgery, was more intense than the pain I had felt after the lumpectomy, and for a few weeks I couldn't bend down over our washer at home to pick up damp clothing at its bottom without feeling like someone was stabbing me in the back of my shoulder with a paring knife.

The medical fellow called. I assumed what had become my traditional "going to get life altering news now" stance and tightly clutched the arm of the chair I was sitting in while holding my breath.

"The results came back for your axillary lymph nodes, and they were negative," he said.

I breathed a sigh of relief so intense I do believe I made our house rattle for a moment. The Powers That Be in the heavens above had finally released their grip on me and I could proceed to the finish line. Now all that awaited me was six weeks of radiation therapy, kicked off by getting punctured in the chest with tiny freckle-like tattoos to outline the treatment fields. Daily undressing and redressing in two johnny gowns and being zapped on a table by a rotating machine became frighteningly routine after just a couple of weeks. Before I knew it, it was graduation day, and I crumpled my worn johnny gowns and tossed them into a laundry bin outside the hospital dressing room for the very last time.

I had a mammography a few months later. The words "nothing suspicious" and "benign tissue" immediately took me back to simpler times, when such a report was the anticipated norm, and something I'd tended to take very much for granted.

Life is for the most part back to being what it was before the cancer diagnosis, with late nights spent sipping lukewarm coffee while calculating and graphing data on my home computer and trying to strengthen proposal aims in time for the next looming grant deadline. Sometimes I forget to take my nightly dose of tamoxifen, but for the most part it's become a reflexive ritual like brushing my teeth or washing my face and I just do it without thinking too hard about the underlying reasons why I'm doing it.

I do have to work harder at combating Lupron- or tamoxifen-related weight gain and am eating a considerably healthier diet with minimal sugar and lots of protein. And some days I feel more fatigued than others and can't figure out why. The office visits every few months with the oncologist and medical fellow are a particularly sobering reminder of what was, and what I will always worry might be again.

And then there are the MRN numbers and patient names and ages and genders that I continue to record in my lab notebook, the bone marrow samples I Ficoll purify and cells I count on a hemocytometer and test the activity of new targeted leukemia drugs against. I will never look at these MRN numbers the same way again.

"You should write about your experiences as a breast cancer patient." I remember one of the technicians said this to me on the day of my last radiation appointment. "I mean, you ladies go through so much," she said.

I nodded. "Yeah, maybe I should."

I agreed it was a journey worth writing about, and in a way, I believe it was a journey that may have taken me to a better place in life. A place where there's more appreciation of who I've been, who I am, and who I still may have the chance to be.

Author Bios

Ken and Ellen launched FACEPAINT, a family-operated 501(c)(3) that provides free educational books/video/film to support social and cultural awareness.

Their publications include short stories and poetry published in the bimonthly literary tabloid, *PKA's Advocate, The Writing Disorder* (quarterly online literary journal and print anthology book), *Unconditionally Her* (formerly *New Focus Daily*), and *Natural Solutions* (formerly *Alternative Medicine Magazine*). The cancer memoir, "From Both

Sides," was published in *Bewildering Stories*. They published several children's/YA books by small presses, including Galde Press and Chipmunkapublishing. These have been widely distributed to schools, public libraries, Little Free Libraries, homeschoolers and parent centers throughout the US and Canada.

FACEPAINT produced the 3D animations, "Justin and the Werloobee," and "Full Moon," based on their published children's stories. Their work strives to promote kindness and empathy, love and friendship.

Ken and Ellen performed for several years as part of a circus troupe. This troupe, also called FACEPAINT, promoted social awareness to Boys and Girls Clubs, retirement homes, and nursing homes throughout New England.

Ken and Ellen live with their daughter, Emily, in Chelmsford, Massachusetts.

An informed, short account of breast cancer treatment.

KIRKUS REVIEW

FROM BOTH SIDES

A MEMOIR

BY ELLEN WEISBERG • RELEASE DATE: NOV. 17, 2022

A leukemia researcher recounts the diagnosis and treatment of her breast cancer.

Weisberg was a researcher at Dana-Farber Cancer Institute, Boston, when she first discovered an abnormality in one of her breasts. Her husband, a pediatrician, reassured her that it felt like a fibroid cyst, but after undergoing investigative procedures, she was told that she had invasive ductal carcinoma. It was also discovered that at least one of her lymph nodes was suspiciously enlarged. The author clearly documents her entire course of care, including taking part in a clinical trial involving a six-month preop combination of hormone therapy and palbociclib, a cancer growth blocker, in an attempt to shrink the tumor. Surgery was then scheduled to remove the tumor, followed by secondary surgery to remove axillary lymph nodes. With the news that her auxiliary lymph nodes tested negative for cancer, Weisberg was given a six-week course of radiation therapy, then a mammogram that showed "nothing suspicious." The memoir opens with an engaging discussion about why people might develop cancer. Weisberg draws on her medical knowledge here but doesn't overwhelm the reader with jargon: "Maybe for certain people, over time, the aging cells, which are constantly dividing and making mistakes that typically get corrected, fail to correct themselves because of a faulty DNA repair system." Readers will appreciate the specifics she shares about her medication: "I know theoretically my tumor—which is 95% progesterone and estrogen receptor-positive—should respond to the tamoxifen and Lupron." She tackles a tough subject with wry humor: "*Is it something other than a tumor? Am I about to give birth any second to an alien baby like in Village of the Damned?*" At 38 pages, the memoir doesn't go into much depth. We do get some glimpses of the author's psychological response to illness; she concludes that her experience with cancer may have given her greater appreciation for life. But this brief work doesn't offer much more than other similar titles.

An informed, short account of breast cancer treatment.

FACEPAINT Nonprofit Books

All Across CANADA
Ellen Weisberg and Ken Yoffe

All Across EUROPE
Ellen Weisberg and Ken Yoffe

All Across CHINA
Ellen Weisberg and Ken Yoffe

Friends and Mates in Fifty States
Ellen Weisberg M.A.   Ken Yoffe M.S.

Angel Rock Leap
Ellen Weisberg
Ken Yoffe

What are microscopes?

Full MOON

Bogs, Swamps and Marshes

GATHERING ROSES
ELLEN WEISBERG

Fruit of the Vine

Making Emmie Smile

https://facepaint.team

FACEPAINT Nonprofit's multi-award-winning
anti-bullying
3D animation, Justin and the Werloobee!

Watch on YouTube!

Made in United States
Orlando, FL
02 October 2023

37492617R00045